100 Doors:

Building Wealth Through Real Estate Cash Flow

By

Andy Dane Carter

Published By

ANDY DANE MEDIA

Andy Dane Media

5062 Lankershim Blvd Ste 2011

North Hollywood, CA 91601

Published by Andy Dane Media

ISBN: 978-0-692-99607-2

Copyright © 2017 Andy Dane Carter

This publication is designed to provide accurate and authoritative information in regard to the subject matter covered. It is sold with the understanding that the publisher is not engaged in rendering legal, accounting, or other professional service. If legal advice or other expert assistance is required, the services of a competent professional person should be sought.

From a declaration of principles jointly adopted by a committee of the American Bar Association and a committee of publishers

INTRODUCTION

"We were not taught financial literacy in school. It takes a lot of work and time to change your thinking and to become financially literate." - Robert Kiyosaki.

The term financial "Financial freedom" is not only reserved for the 1% of the world. It is not reserved for only the wealthy. Financial freedom is reserved for the people that take the time, effort and energy to take control of their investment future and their financial future by learning how to buy positive cash flow assets. It is the number one way I invest and it's the only way I invest in real estate.

The skill set that I will teach you in my book, Hundred Doors, will give you the blueprint and the outline to take control of your financial future, your family's financial future and give you the opportunity to have generational wealth transfer. It doesn't matter if you make $20,000 a year or you make $20,000,000 a year. These proven concepts and proven philosophies have made myself, my family, my investors and many clients a lot of money over the years. These are proven concepts that have worked well before I was here. I've just simplified the game, so hopefully everybody can have a little bit of what I have.

First and foremost, I am passionate about people and real estate. I am committed to helping people thrive in their business and investment power, so they can be in alignment with their success mindset. My Unlock Now program and my Hundred Doors book is the platform to support your mindset with the knowledge that gains you leverage to your true potential for investing in your legacy.

For me, real estate is fun. It's exciting, it's scary, it's all those things all rolled into one. It's an amazing way to build wealth, generational wealth, that could change your children's-children's lives. I have successfully bought, sold, built, developed, flipped, held for myself and my investors over half a billion dollars in real estate. This is my passion and I love what I do.

I have done this in the real estate game from deals that are 30 to 40,000 all the way up to multi-million-dollar investment projects and development deals and everything in between, but my biggest accomplishment is not my financial success, it's not how much money I have and it's not how many commas and zeros I have in the bank and it sure isn't about how many properties I own. My biggest accomplishment is my family.

I am a husband and I am a dad to two amazing boys, Jackson and Grayson Carter. They are the light of my life. They are my "Why". I love my family deeply. I am very blessed and extremely grateful for everything that I have. I am extremely grateful for everywhere that I've been and everywhere that I'm going.

For me, staying in a state of continuous gratitude is the key to my success. I work extremely hard, but I also turn my phone on airplane mode twice a day. This is crucial to my work-life balance. From 5 p.m. to 8 p.m., my phone goes on airplane mode. No text, no emails, no social media, no conference calls, nothing. Just family. Just me at home with my kids and my wife playing, doing whatever we do as a family. Then from 8 p.m. to 10 p.m. I turn my phone back off to airplane mode and finish out the day. Then I do the same thing in the morning. I wake up, morning meditation, I sit in gratitude for five minutes, I work out, then I make my family breakfast every morning and then I turn my phone on. I step into my day. I don't let my day come at me. It is crucial for the time management to have a successful life.

I am deeply honored to bring you this book Hundred Doors and give you a glimpse into my life, where I've been, what I've done and how hopefully I can help you shift your mindset into a success mindset. I can help you unlock your true potential, so you can step into your full power. I hope you enjoy this amazing book and blueprint, The Hundred Doors.

Andy Dane Carter

ANDYDANECARTER.COM

TABLE OF CONTENTS

Chapter One:

FIRST
REAL ESTATE DEAL

My first real estate deal I ever closed personally was for an investor. When I set out to get into real estate I always knew I was going to work with investors and become an investor as well one day. My first deal I ever did was a property that a particular group of investors had bought at the auction. They paid cash for it at the court steps, and it was a property that was in pretty bad shape, and it was vacant. So, once they closed I got an email with the property address, and I went over there, and I checked it out.

An Unusual Request

I called our lockout crew to secure the property, and when I got to the property there was a very sweet old lady, probably in her, I don't know, 80s, that was sitting on the porch next door, and I waved and said hi, and she was very friendly, and she said, "Oh, you know what's going on, you know, with the property?"

I said, "Oh, you know, it just sold, and it's going to be, you know, completely fixed up, and, you know it's going to look beautiful, and it's going to get remodeled." The lady said, "Well, you know what? My sister who's quite a bit younger really wants to buy it, so how much are they going to ask for it if they don't do any of the rehab, and they don't fix it up at all?"

I said, "Well, that's a very good question." I went to the investors, and I said I possibly have a potential buyer of the property that we just bought today.

We don't have to do anything like rehab; we don't have to even hammer a nail. So, I took down the lady's information, and I drove back and forth to meet with her personally over the next week; probably about seven or eight times, and then I met with her sister, and I got her sister pre-approved with a preferred lender, and within 30 days a property that we had bought, we had sold.

Lesson Learned

We bought it below market. We sold it for below market to them, and my first real estate deal I ever did I found my buyer sitting on the front porch of the house next door; so, you never know where you buyer is going to come from, but my first real estate transaction was dealing with an 80 something year old very sweet lady, and her sister who was in her early 70s, and they didn't do email. They didn't DocuSign. They had a land line at the house, so I did a lot of driving with contracts back and forth from escrow and lenders, and I spent a small fortune of time and gas driving back and forth from San Pedro. But they were very excited they got the property.

My investor was able to make a nice little profit without having to do any rehab to the property what so ever; so, my first real estate transaction was an investment purchase from the court steps that I was able to sell to the neighbor's sister, and they are very, very excited, and I believe still live there today.

That was my first real estate transaction.

Chapter Two:

8
PRINCIPLES

Over the years I have come to realize there have been eight core principles to my investing success in real estate. As you go on your real estate investing journey use these principles as guide to help you navigate through.

Principle Number One.

Cash Flow Is King.

This is a pretty simple concept. If a property cash flows, I.e., your renters or your tenants are bringing in more income than the mortgage. For example, if your mortgage is roughly $4200 and your monthly income from the property is 5000, you are cash flowing $800 before expenses. That property is cash flowing, that property will give you the freedom to enjoy steady monthly income. You can grow, you can expand. You can build an empire from one piece of property. You can slowly build over five, 10, 20, 30 years wealth

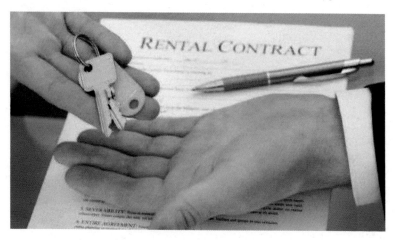

beyond your wildest dreams, all through cash flow. Cash flow is king. It is the number one principle, in my opinion, for investing in real estate to hold long term for wealth growth.

Principle Number Two.

Use Positive Leverage To Your Advantage.

What this means is you want your money to grow and you want your wealth to grow and expand while you sleep. You want to make money 24/7. The only way to really do that is investing long term with real estate where you get good debt, not bad debt. You use good positive leverage, not negative leverage that keeps you up at night. So, what I mean by that is cash flow creates an opportunity for positive leverage. Positive leverage is you taking out a loan for a piece of property. Let's say it's 400,000, your down payment is roughly 100,000. Well, you're controlling a $400,000 piece of real estate for only $100,000. If that piece of real estate goes up 10%, 15%, 20% over four or five years, your $100,000 just made you 200,000, 300,000. Maybe you pull out some of it and buy another piece of property, so you use positive leverage, not negative leverage.

Principle Number Three.

Stay True To Who You Are.

I can't stress this enough. If you are the kind of person that loves to save and you're a saver. There's nothing wrong with that. But you need to know who you are and where your thresholds are for risk. Some people like to bet it all and see what happens. Some people like to bet a little and see what happens and if they win, maybe put some money in their pocket and then bet again. You really have to know who you are when investing long term in real estate. It's going to help you buy properties quicker. It's going to help you buy properties in a much more sound manner where you get to sleep well at night. The whole purpose of buying and holding real estate long term is to give you this freedom. If you're not buying real estate in alignment with who you are as a person, it's going to create stress in your life instead of the freedoms and joys that it's created in my life. I get to do whatever I want because I know who I am, I know how risk adverse I need to be. I know how I'm wired. I also know that if a property's not cash flowing, it stresses me out, so I only buy properties that cash flow.

Principle Number Four.

Set Goals And Targets For Your Investment Strategies.

You need to know exactly what you want, roughly where it's at, and how to go get it. The way to get leverage on yourself is for you set a goal and you put yourself into motion. For example, by Wednesday at 2:00 p.m. I'm going to have made five phone calls to five different real estate brokers and have a conversation with them letting them know I'm a real estate investor, would you like to represent me, this is what I'm trying to accomplish, do you have anything in your inventory that might fit what I'm looking for, here's what I'm prequalified for. You give yourself a definitive time to get something done. You set strategic investment targets and then you put your plan into motion and you execute.

Principle Number Five.

Look For The Opportunities.

I can't tell you how many times I've purchased a piece of real estate that came to me via third and fourth party from somebody who knew somebody that they told somebody that I invest in real estate. You never know where your next deal's at. You never know where it's going to come from. It could come from a friend of a friend at a cocktail party and you guys just so happen to be talking about real estate and they say, "Oh, you know what? We have this duplex that we've had in our family forever and we're looking to get rid of it. Would you mind coming over and maybe taking a look at it and writing us an offer?" Or you could be in a meeting talking about something completely different and you happen to bring up real estate and somebody happens to tell you, "Oh, hey you know what? I just bought this piece of real estate. I'm not really sure what to do with it. I think I'm going to wholesale it. Do you want to take a look at it?" Sure. When you position yourself as a real estate investor, it opens up a lot of possibilities and a lot of opportunities for you to at least get a look at a property when maybe you wouldn't have before.

Principle Number Six.
Invest On Principles, Not Emotion.

That is just the real estate game. It's a real estate game. It is an investment game. If you play the game with emotion, you can get emotionally destroyed. You invest on the numbers. If the numbers make sense, you do the deal. If the numbers don't make sense, but it's your dream property and it's got all the things you've always wanted to put in your portfolio, so you can tell all your friends, "Look at this gorgeous property I have" and it's not going to cash flow for 10 years. Take the emotion out.

Principle Number Seven.

Surround Yourself With People That Can Take You To The Next Level.

This has helped me grow in this field exponentially. I surrounded myself with investors, with mentors. I hired coaches. I hired mentors. I read tons of books. I submerged myself in this environment, as well as the industry. I wanted to be around people that had already been where I wanted to go. So, I invested a lot of time and a lot of money in getting educated before I bought my first property. This, for me, was crucial. It took a lot of the guess work completely out of it and they were able to help me with some of the very hard decisions and I'm really glad they did. It has given me the freedom that I have today. Surround yourself with people that can take you to the next level and share your vision.

Principle Number Eight.

Maximize Your Time.

Time is the one thing we can't get back. Time is the one thing that is the even playing field. Mark Zuckerberg, Gary Vaynerchuk, all the owners of big companies, billion-dollar companies, all get the same 24 hours. It's how you use that 24 hours that's going to differentiate you from your friends and your business partners and your family and where you want to go. Time is our greatest asset. So, spend time maximizing your time with your properties that you own. One of the easiest ways to increase rent is paint and landscape. You make the outside and the inside nice, clean, new paint, new landscape, new facelift and you have a nice piece of property to rent for a little expense and you can come to market for higher rent. Spend your time with your existing properties. Don't always just be on the hunt. Make sure as you acquire properties, you get them to their highest and best use. You get them to full market value. You put in the time and money to maximize that particular asset in your portfolio. It will pay dividends for years and years and years. Take care of your properties, take care of your tenants and they will take care of you beyond your wildest dreams.

Lesson Learned

In closing, real estate investing is a lifestyle for work, life, balance. If you want to spend all your time investing and chasing a deal and not enjoying time at home, enjoying time with your family, taking vacations, working out, eating well, and celebrating your wins; well, then, you've lost. The whole point of investing in real estate is kind of worthless because then you're just doing it for the money. The money's great. The money gives you a sense of stability and a sense of accomplishment and a sense of freedom. Those are all great. Let me just tell you, life is not about how much money you put in the bank, but it's how much life you truly get to live.

Chapter Three:

FIRST DEAL
I CLOSED FOR A
CLIENT

My first real estate deal that I closed for a client/friend of mine that was in the traditional sense of real estate.

Acting As The Listing Agent

Actually, I was the listing agent for a condo on Ocean in Long Beach, and it was a two-bedroom, one bath condo in a very nice building, and it had two parking spots which is always nice for Long Beach parking. It is a little hard to get in Long Beach. Long Beach is a parking impacted city, so condominiums that are on Ocean that have views of the ocean with two parking spots, and it's a two-bedroom, one bath are very, very desirable.

At the time I think the price was right around $230,000, $240,000, so it is a very good price point for first time home buyers, or people who are looking to invest in real estate, and they buy the condos, they fix them up, and they get top rent for them as an investment property, which you can get into the market for a very reasonable price.

Selling In A Down Market

So, my first one I did was this condo, and it was in a down market. It was like in the beginning of the crash, and I was able to get an all cash buyer for $30,000 over list, and we were able to close it in ten days, and I had a very happy client. She was a retired professor from Long Beach state, and a dear friend of mine; so, I was glad I was able to help her out.

She was living in San Diego at the time, and wanted to liquidate her condo, and I was able do it for a discounted commission which I always like to do, and I was able to help her get that done, and she was very, very grateful that we were able to get it done so quickly, and I even had one of my crews who disposes of a lot of trash and debris for all of our properties all over Los Angeles drive up and help her move, and get everything out of the property. So, it was stripped and ready for demolition for the investor that bought it, so everybody was very, very thrilled how the transaction went, and how the property was left.

Going The Extra Mile

That can be a little bit of a problem sometimes. The people leave things behind. They leave debris, but when you have a list of people that you can go to that makes everybody's life much, much easier, and adds tremendous amount of value to what you bring to the table as a professional, so if someone says, "Hey, do you have a plumber?" I have six. Or, "Do you have a good floor guy?" I have a handful, so I keep a very deep rolodex of people that might be able to help my clients, might be able to help me, my investors.

Lesson Learned

So, my condo transaction was the first transaction that I did for a client in the traditional sense of real estate outside of the investing world that I was entrenched in, and it was the first condo I had ever listed and sold as well, so I got to learn some of the ins and outs of CC&Rs and HOAs and different things you need to walk through when you're selling a condo versus a regular traditional piece of residential real estate like in single family residence.

Chapter Four:

THE POWER
OF MULI-FMAILY UNITS

The power of transitioning into multi-family units, apartment units, apartment buildings, is such a great way to head to the market. Because even if the stock market implodes, and even if the housing market crashes, your tenants will still be paying for your asset. Your tenants will still be paying your mortgage. So, even if you lose equity, i.e., let's say you bought the property for 400 it goes up to 600, the market takes a dive and it falls all the way down to, like, 420, well, you're still making money, you're still cash flowing, you're still making income off your property from your tenants paying your mortgage, and this can sustain the drought. They're able to sustain the lull and the crash when they move into the correction and when you're in the correction phase, that's when you do a little sprucing up. Maybe you do some new paint and landscape and then you get a better return on your investment and you can increase the rents which will dramatically increase your gross rent.

Why It Simply Makes Sense

Multiply; which I will explain later in the book, these are all things why real estate makes so much sense. If you invest in a company, per se, and that company takes a dive, or they take a 50% loss or half of what they produce got lost in shipping or you had a humongous recall, so your fourth quarter earnings are down 30 percent and your stock just took a dive. Those problems don't happen to investors that are holding in real estate, that are holding investments, and especially once you're in a commercial space, then you start owning the ware houses, the strip malls; these places where people have businesses and companies, they go to you to run their company and then they pay you rent.

All of the billionaires and hundreds of millionaires in the world have a foothold in real estate for a reason. So, let's say there were people who make millions and millions in business part their money, part their wealth, it is the bank for the rich. There's amazing tax benefits of holding for the long term, there's amazing benefits to owning real estate that you buy for 100,000 and in 20 years, sell it for a million or even give it to your children or you transfer it to your trust. If you study the history of real estate, anything it holds for any amount of time is given a net easier to reach to get to its return. Yes, you can say these things for some of the stock and some of the very, very long, old school customers who have been around for a long time, but nothing is as tried and true. You buy it, you hold it, you maintain it, you profit from it.

Working With Professionals

There is the end. I have helped hundreds and hundreds of people do this. Some of them are doctors, some of them are lawyers, some of them are just regular people that work for regular companies. I helped a buddy of mine who is a general manager for a crane leasing company, you know, because he wanted to make a difference for his family, so he wanted to take his money out of the stock market and put it into real estate. He's like, I bought my house, my house went up, I made 300,000, how can I do this on a larger scale? We put a plan together, execute it. Regular guy.

So, there's so many ways to get into the real estate investment space. It's about unlocking a belief system, it's about unlocking a mental capability that you maybe didn't have before. Investing in real estate is not this get rich quick thing. Yes, you can flip properties and yes you can make money quickly. But if you really want to be wealthy and you really want the long game and you want the generational shift; then, you will have to consider this plan-even if you are flipping houses, hey! I still do 40, 50 a year. We used to do hundreds, but you take the cash you make from flipping properties and you put them into really good, long term loans for leverage. Good leverage and you buy good real estate.

A Prime Example

So, let's say you make 200,000 in flipping, go buy a property. Put 200,000 down and then repeat so every year you flip properties to buy yourself a larger building and larger assets. In five years, you're a millionaire. And not one million, like, millions. So, it's all possible. I did it and I'm helping other people do it. I've helped tons of people unlock a new story. To help them tell themselves a new story around what real estate really looks like and once you start really diving into this language, because real estate is a language, it becomes fun and exciting and with the fun and exciting, the fears begin to lift, because you start to understand.

It's Within Your Reach

It's not some big scary monster that's only for the one percent. In my opinion it's the greatest way to become part of the one percent, especially from somebody like me who got c's, d's and f's in school; I would rather work, you know, than get all that stuff done, but when I found and discovered the ridiculous possibilities of buying and holding real estate and having my tenants pay for my life style, pay for the life I have on in my home, at my office. Having my tenants pay for my small kids to go to private school and taking that burden off me, is amazing; like, they just pay the way.

Lesson Learned

So, I do love my tenants, I have a lot of respect for them and I take great care of them. I get Christmas cards from my tenants. I'm a good landlord, I have an amazing property management team. These are all really important things you consider when building a team of professionals around you; so, when you buy it, you buy it correctly and then you have another team of incredible professionals that run your empire for you, even if your empire is one duplex. That's where you start. It's all possible. You've just gotta give yourself permission to understand a new belief system.

Chapter Five:

EIGHT MYTHS
OF REAL ESTATE

These eight real estate myths kept me stuck for years until I unlocked these myths from my subconscious. I was running, and I was operating my own companies and didn't have my head fully around the value and the net worth of real estate and real estate investing. When I began to unlock these myths that don't always give you the courage to open the door, nor does it give you the ability to walk through the doorway without fear, I began to see my real estate investing in a new light. It is the first step in unlocking a potentially new room, new adventure, new path, and new opportunities.

Change Your Belief System

I invite you in to this new belief system about real estate. Real estate investing and building generational wealth through real estate and real estate investment properties to hold long-term. I'd like to offer you that maybe what you have thought about real estate and real estate investing just might not be true. May I have you consider that there might be an easier, softer way to build long-term wealth and generational wealth transfers through real estate and real estate investing? Let's begin.

Myth Number One.

I Don't Need A Real Estate Agent Or Broker To Do My Real Estate Transactions.

Yes, the lone wolf approach is possible, but I don't advise it. I advise surrounding yourself with professionals, experts in their fields, and like-minded individuals trying to get you the highest returns for your money and sitting down with a professional and getting a clear vision on what you're trying to accomplish by investing in real estate, what your goals are, short-term and long-term, and the best way to execute.

I strongly urge you to shift your mindset from average; especially when you're starting out. The fears will creep in because you don't know much about this particular industry, and you will come from an average mindset. Try to put yourself in a mindset of a seasoned professional real estate investor while you are trying to gain information and data to really get your head around the best way to execute your plans. Everything you've ever wanted is on the other side of fear; once you walk through the door, the fear door of real estate investing. I can only tell you it is incredible on the other side.

Myth Number Two.

Oh, I Don't Know Much About Real Estate, So I Couldn't Possibly Be Successful In It.

Wrong. You need to believe in yourself. When I became a wine sommelier at 21, which is an expert in wine, when I first started in that particular field, I knew there was white wine, red wine, and pink wine. Fast forward 24 months, I could smell a glass of wine and tell you what kind of grape it was, what country it came from, what region within that country it came from, and the vintage, the year which it was produced by looking at it, smelling it, and tasting it. So, it is possible to get on the fast-track to the level of expert in any field if you put your mind to it and you change your story and you change your belief system around what you can accomplish.

Myth Number Three.

I Only Have $10,000 To Invest, So I Couldn't Possibly Ever Buy A Property.

Really? Wrong. You don't have to have a ton of money in the bank to buy and close on a piece of real estate. Yes, you need cash. Yes, you need capital or access to it, but again, I want you to get your head around a new belief system of how can I make this work? How could I possibly execute this? Could I maybe work with a real estate broker? Could I maybe have him or her throw in some of their commission to help offset my down payment? Could I try to find a deal myself and bring that to a seasoned investor and tell them, "Hey, you know what? I'd like to split this with you. Would you be willing to split the deal with me?"

There's a lot of different ways to get into the real estate market with a little bit of money or no money. Or you find a really good lender, you find some way to get into the real estate market with hard money that makes sense for you financially. There's a ton of ways to execute, but you have to give yourself the option of it might be a different way than just your conventional 20 to 25% down, you spend your entire life savings, and then you wait. There is an easier, softer way. You have to hustle. You have to grind, and you have to continually try to educate yourself and get more knowledge on how to make it happen.

Myth Number Four.

I Should Only Invest In The Areas Where I Live.

Yes. This is a very, very good piece of advice. At the same time, it's not the only way. Now, as we speak, at the time of this recording, the California real estate market, the southern California real estate market, is on fire. It's extremely hard to get real estate, and it's really expensive; so, I have gone out of state. I have six duplexes. Six. Six duplexes right now in escrow that I am about to close on that for all six are 260,000. For all six duplexes, that cash flow about four to $5,000 a month. Where I live in southern California, you can barely buy a little teeny tiny condo that's not going to cash flow at all for that price point. So I use the same principles, the same methods that I would do here in southern California, and I'm executing it in Pittsburgh or Arizona or Ohio. It doesn't matter. The principles always apply. You find good property managers. You do your due diligence. You surround yourself with real estate professionals, and you execute.

Myth Number Five.

I Will Leave The Real Estate Investigations And Due Diligence To My Real Estate Agent Or My Broker.

Wrong. This could possibly be catastrophic. You want to be at the tip of the spear. You want to do all of your own due diligence. You want to do all of your own research. You want to go to the city. You want to pull the file for that piece of property that the city has. You want to know if there's any liens on it. Is there any violations? Was there any construction that went sideways? You want to ask a million questions because the more information you have, the better and well-rounded the real estate deal will be. You will feel more confident because you've asked all the questions, but you can't rely on your real estate agent or broker to ask all of the questions that you need for your piece of real estate. It's your job to do your due diligence and take responsibility for your investment.

Myth Number Six.

I'm Going To Wait For The Market To Get Better Before I Buy.

This is just flat out, not true. I buy real estate in good markets, bad markets, markets that are going up, and markets that are going down because I have a very simple method. It's cash flow. Does the property cash flow? How much cash flow can I make in the shortest period of time? So, it doesn't matter if the property is going up in value or going down in value. What matters to me the most is will the tenants that are in my property more than cover my mortgage? And what does that number look like? Cash flow is everything, in a good market or a bad market. It does not matter.

Myth number seven.

The best brokers and agents are the ones that drive the nice fancy cars, that work for the nice, big brokerages, and that look like they are extremely wealthy. This just isn't true. I work with all kinds of different real estate professionals. I work with trust attorneys. I work with brand new real estate agents that have never done a deal, to men and women who have been in the real estate game for 40, 50 years and everything in between. I look at the deal and I try to position myself with all kinds of people. I like people, and you

never know where your next deal is going to come from. I get deals from people in my office. "Hey, my mom's cousin is looking to sell the family's apartment building. Would you be interested in taking a look?" Sure. You never know where your next opportunity is going to lie, so if you position yourself and you present yourself as a real estate investor or somebody who acquires real estate, you will build a network that will turn into a vacuum. When that happens, let me just tell you. It's incredible.

Myth Number Eight.

Finally, We Come To Myth Number Eight. Cash Flow Is Only For The Wealthy Real Estate Investor.

Wrong. Yes, while cash is king, and cash flow is the only way I buy investment real estate, it is not only for the super-seasoned investor. It is for the mom and dad. It is for the teacher. It is for the doctor, the lawyer, the student just coming out of college. It is for everybody. If the property cash flows, it removes a massive amount of risk. It doesn't remove all of the risk, but it removes a very large chunk of it.

A High School Teacher

A story I like to tell is a story of the teacher at the high school right around the corner from where I grew up. The most she ever made in an entire year was $30,000, and she retired a millionaire, because she bought a piece of real estate every five years for 30 years. Nothing big. Nothing flashy. Nothing hard, but she consistently stuck to her plan, and she retired with millions in equity and in the bank. One of my favorite stories.

Lesson Learned

Cash flow is for everybody. If you find cash flow and you find a property that cash flows and the numbers make sense, you do the deal. If you're going to lose four, $500 a month, sometimes you do the deal, but for the most part, 99% of the time, I don't do it. If it cash flows and it makes sense, I acquire it and put it in my portfolio. Cash flow is king.

Chapter Six:

UNDERSTANDING
THE PROPERTY GRADING SYSTEM

We'll start with the A. The A is exactly what it sounds like. It's a grade A. It's the best. Everything is done. It is an A+ property. Those A+ properties usually have top rents. You get the A+ rent. You get the highest rents in the area. I want to give you an example of what an A property looks like and a personal experience I had with an A property with one of my investors.

My A Graded Property Experience

One of my investors loves a particular style of real estate. It is a 1930's Spanish, really rustic-looking type of architecture. In a certain area in southern California on the beach there are quite a few of these. She's always wanted one. She's always wanted one as an investment property. She's always wanted that marquee property. We found one. It came to market. It had just been fully rehabbed, fully remodeled, was gorgeous, fully historically restored. No penny was wasted. They spent tons of money fully restoring this property even down to the little tiny Spanish tiles that wove down the cement spiral staircase that slowly cascaded down to the courtyard. This property was gorgeous, absolutely gorgeous and fully remodeled.

New kitchen, new bath, the only thing they kept was some of the historical fixtures, the historical, beautiful hardwood floors that got refinished, all new plumbing, all new electric, new roof, new windows except for the ones that were historic. They had to actually have those reconstructed. Beautiful, beautiful, A+ property selling at the top of the market. It was a four-unit, big, nice, large four-plex on the beach.

Beautiful property. I was able to secure the property for my investor and there were 12 people that were trying to get it, 12 other offers. My firm and I were able to get it locked up for them at just over list price, which was, I think, right around $2.5 million.

The potential buyers, my clients, were thrilled, and super excited. She was going to get this beautiful dream property. It was an A. We got it. We did our inspections. There was barely anything wrong with it. Everything was perfect. It was brand new. It was going to get the top market rent, but she had paid top market value for it and so on. She found one of the best property management teams in the entire city to manage it for her. It got fully occupied at the top market rents. Everything was said and done. Escrow closed. It's cash flowing right around $400 a month. It still meets all of the minimum requirements for my strategies that I use with my investors and myself. It cash flows. The cash flows $400 a month.

I Invest Differently

The tenants are covering the mortgage plus expenses. What's left over is the cash flow. They are cash flow positive $400 a month. She has this beautiful, Spanish, gorgeous piece of real estate. She's happy. I'm happy that she's happy, but it's not the way I choose to invest. It's not the way I choose to spend my family's money. It's very difficult to get more out of your property when everything's already been done.

Why I Invest Differently

For example, if you have an A property you can't go in and remodel the kitchen and add value. It's already done. You can't go in and raise rents because your rents are already at the top of the market. You can maybe get a 2%, 3% kick sometimes a year or 2, and because they bought the property 4 years ago and it's a really good market here in southern California, they've

made about $300,000, $400,000 on their investment, which is good, but that's the appreciation game. They're playing the appreciation game of real estate, which means they're going to hold the thing hopefully indefinitely and they watch their money slowly climb up the mountain.

A Graded Property Vacancies

The problem is if you have vacancies for one or two months when you're at the top of the heap, you have to start digging into your own pocket. That's something that doesn't really work for me and my strategies for my family; but it works great for them and their family. That's what an A property looks like, but if you're trying to refinish or go back and do some rehab to increase the property value of an A property it might take you a while to do so because everything's already done. It's the best. Everything's perfect. Most rents you can possibly get, everything is done. Maintenance is very, very low because everything's brand new, which is a good thing if you want an A property.

Understanding B Graded Properties

Now, B properties are sometimes hard to tell if it's a B or an A. You can usually tell based on zip code or where it is. Is it next to a school or a college? Is it next to a downtown area? Is it next to where there's some cool things going on, some restaurants and shops? They can look similar to an A but maybe they're a B just because they're a little bit further in from the coast or they're a little bit pushed out from where the downtown area is. It depends on the demographic of where you live and where you invest.

An Example Of A B Graded Property

I'll give you an example of a B property that I helped another friend of mine actually acquire in east Los Angeles, a very cool, hip zone, very up and coming. We got her a three-unit triplex. The way the property was laid out, it was a little two-bedroom, one-bath house in the front, really cool 1930-something craftsman, all wood, had a front porch, really, really just cute and cool. Long driveway down the side of the property and three one-car garages in the back with two-bedroom, one-bath units above the garages. It was maybe two or three blocks in from a very hip area where there's tons of restaurants and coffee shops and all kinds of places to do yoga and listen to music. It was in a really cool, hip, new zone of Los Angeles.

This was a B property because she bought it from an investor. The investor had done a lot of the work. They didn't do it all, did about 85%. We were able to close escrow on it. It needed landscape. It needed some paint. We did that. She put in some raised beds in the back, so she could have veggies and herbs and stuff like that. We put in a really cool wood fence in the front and made it really hip and just finished some of the things that the investor didn't quite do all the way to almost make it almost an A property.

How It Cash Flowed

She was able to increase the rents by right around $50 a door, which isn't a lot but it was something. She was able to increase her value by a small margin. In the past two years she's made a little bit of money. She hasn't quite got to the gross rent multiplier that she wanted to because she's pretty close to top market rent and she doesn't have quite enough money to afford a long vacancy period for one of her units. She likes to keep the rents just a little bit lower. This beautiful triplex in a really cool, hip area of Los Angeles is a really good example of what a B property can be. You do some paint. You do a little bit of landscape. You dress it up a little bit, but this property already had new bathrooms. It already had new kitchens. A big chunk of the work had already been done by the investor to up the value of the property in the eyes of the bank if you're trying to refinance out on cash and do another project, but again, my client, my investor was very happy.

The Difference Of B, C, & D

This is the kind of property she wanted. That's what we found for her. That's what we executed on. She's thrilled. Her margins and her business model, everything was met. Really cool craftsman triplex, it's got everything she wanted in a pride of ownership scenario for a landlord and for an investor. That's what a B property looks like. I'll dive deeper into why I invest in C and D and sometimes even F properties because I can get my money, my cash on cash out of the property quicker by adding value quickly. What I mean by that is when I go in and put in new kitchens, new bathrooms and I redo it and I do most of the investor kind of work and I take the rents from $800 a month to $1,400 a month, I dramatically change the gross rent multiplier that the banks look at for added value. I take a property that might be $400,000. I put in $60,000. I raise all the rents and now I'm in for 460, but now the property is worth almost 7. Now I have a very different asset on my hands.

Difference Between Asset Building Versus Real Estate Investing

It's an asset I can hold, I can sell, I can flip, I can refinance the cash out so my cash on cash is zero. My tenants are covering all of my mortgage, all of my refinance cost, closing. Everything is covered by the tenants. I'm still going to cash flow. These are strategies and metrics that are so important to live by, which is why I only invest on metrics. I only invest on the numbers. I don't get emotionally attached to the piece of real estate. I look at the numbers and how I can make my money back the fastest and still provide a great place for somebody to live which is why I personally don't buy A and B properties, because there's not enough room for me to do what I do for my family to increase our net worth and try to expand what I'm teaching my two young boys how to do.

The Properties I like

I try to find properties that do need work because that's the way I can go back to the bank and say, "Here's what I bought the property for. Here's what I've done. It's been reassessed at this particular value. May I kindly have my money back," in a nutshell. Then I can continue. Then I take that capital and I try to go do it again. It sounds like a simple formula because it really is. It's a simple formula. Like most things, it's simple but not easy. If you execute on it and you stick to your guns and you stick to your numbers, you can dramatically increase your wealth over five to ten years, and that'll change your grandkids' grandkids trajectory. This is why I love real estate with every atom in my body. There's just so much upside.

Where I Came From

When I was living in a one-bedroom apartment, living out of a cooler with my little brother and my mom, trust me, I didn't think any of this was possible. I didn't think it was possible through my teen years. I've been diagnosed with severe dyslexia. No one told me anything about, oh; I can maybe do this real estate. As I go into the corporate world, nobody told me anything about real estate. As I learned, I put all my chips in and I really went to work on learning how to educate myself on how to invest in my family's future. I was told same thing as everybody else, go get a really good job, work really hard, put your money in the stock market and mutual funds, and invest for the long-term, until my mutual fund got cut in half after I'd been putting money in since I was 19 years old. I realized that I was very, very exposed. It felt terrible. I felt I had an obligation to myself to take control of my financial future. I did so with the avenues of real estate. I'm really glad I have.

I'll get much deeper into why I buy C and D properties and why they are so lucrative and can be so beneficial for you and your family in the next chapter.

Chapter Seven:

WHY I CHOOSE
C & D PROPERTIES

The reason why I'm a huge fan of C and D grade properties and sometimes I dip into the F's, but those are the ones that need a lot of love, but sometimes you get some great returns there, is that the C and the D properties really give me and my team and my investors and my family an opportunity to add value to the particular asset, to add value to the piece of real estate, to add value to the neighborhood, to add value to the community, to add value to the new tenant and to add value to my company and add value across the board. Our play as investors is to value add as fast as possible, to extract back out of the asset our cash and capital so we can reinvest it and do the same thing all over again.

Knowing Why It's Important To Add Value

What I mean by that is the quicker I can make the piece of real estate, the quicker I can make the particular building worth more money, the quicker the bank will let me refinance it and I can get my particular cash on cash capital back out of the property again to go do it again. For example, next I'll speak about the C properties. Now, C properties are almost my favorite. D's are my favorite. C's are pretty close and sometimes it just varies on how they might be able to scale a little bit quicker, solely based on what's going on with the city, what's going on in the particular neighborhood. All these things are really, really important to take into consideration.

I buy very heavy in C and D neighborhoods. I buy really aggressively in C and D neighborhoods that are right next to B neighborhoods that are moving towards a different class and a different asset class. What I mean by that is when a certain neighborhood is starting to shift, is starting to move in a direction where there's more businesses, there's more commerce, there's more going on, which will help increase the value of the property. For example, if there was a D property that was right next to maybe a B class neighborhood, then if I can do a certain amount of renovation that particular D asset will be a B much faster, solely based on what's happening around that particular building or that particular neighborhood is helping push the values up.

C Building Example

For example, I bought a C building for my family. This particular building was eight units. It was in south Orange County, which is in southern California. It wasn't in the greatest neighborhood, but it wasn't in the worst neighborhood. It was in that in-between land. It just so happened to be next to a college. Now, that's a particular tip of mine I like to always tell people. It's really good to look at real estate that's in a close proximity to a college because you're going to have a lot of people that are going to need rents and rentals for years and years and years. They're really good assets to hold. I bought this particular building. It needed a lot. It was probably more like a C-. It was almost D building. It needed a new roof. It needed a lot of stuff. It needed some new plumbing. It needed new electrics. It needed new windows. One of the units was rehabbed not too bad, but most of the tenants were eight to ten-year long-term tenants, which is good but the good thing for me was their rents were ridiculously below market.

My Vision Of The Property

When I was able to acquire the building, I knew even before I hammered one nail, before I put on any new paint, before I did anything to upgrade the physical structure of the building, the physical structure of the asset to make it worth more money, I knew I was already ahead of the game because there was so much room for me to increase the value solely based on when I increased the rents. People have been living there for years and years and years well below market. Market rent was somewhere around $1,600 a door. They were paying $600, $750. They were grossly under market. It was an incredible deal. I closed it very, very quickly.

The first thing I did was that I sent my team over there and we let everybody know what was going to be going on, that the building had changed hands and there was going to be some construction going on, on a couple of the units that were vacant and that rents were going to be raised. There's certain laws that it depends on where you live and where you're at and how you can raise the rents, but some of the tenants got really upset. They were going to leave. I told every single one of them, "You are more than happy to stay, but if you don't want to pay this amount of rent, no problem at all." It was a very slight increase from where they were at, which was still grossly below market value, because if I kept them in the unit that meant I didn't have to rehab the unit and I couldn't raise the rent a little bit and be fair. I always like to be fair with people.

That's what I did with some of the tenants. Some of the tenants left, which actually worked out in my favor because then I was able to rehab and remodel those particular units at a slower rate and I didn't have to do the entire building at once, which was great. The particular tenants that stayed and their rent went up a few hundred dollars per door, I was able to dramatically increase the gross rent multiplier of that building, which was great because I'd almost hit my number before I'd hammered any nails. By the time I was finished rehabbing that C- property ... It took me a while. It took me probably three months longer than I anticipated. It was almost a nine-month project, but the upside was so incredible that I was able to refinance my money completely out within the first year. It was amazing.

More Upside For Me

I was able to rehab the units from the tenants that didn't want to stay and pay the increased rent. I was able to pull those brand-new units up to $1,600 a door, which was double what they were getting before. I was able to work with the tenants that stayed and slowly rehab their units and that was very easy and comfortable for them and their family. Once they realized I was a good guy and I wasn't there just to raise everybody's rents and I was actually making the property nicer, some of the tenants that didn't really like me in the beginning actually thanked me for the work I had done on the property. They had thanked me for building a brand-new facility with brand new washer and dryers. They thanked me for building this beautiful large area that's all full of grass and there's a grill and a barbecue, this incredible place for them to come and hang out. They thanked me for putting the fence around the entire property; so, now they had some privacy. They thanked me for repaving all of their parking spots.

Be A Good Landlord, Avoid The Slumlord Mentality

Sometimes when you go into these properties people are mad because they're afraid of change, but if you come in as a slumlord and you come in as a bad guy and you just want more money, it's just a bad place to be. If you treat people good and you're improving the property ... This is in my portfolio for my family. I try to keep my tenants very, very happy. The longer they stay and the happier they are, the more they continue to pay for my asset. They pay for my family's wealth. I treat them well. I thank them. I send them Christmas cards. I made the property very, very nice. I was able to go back to the bank. I was able to ridiculously increase the value of the property in a very short period of time, which allowed me to extract my entire cash on cash investment including all of my rehab costs, all within 12 months.

Now, that particular asset, that particular building is running like a well-oiled company. The tenants are happy. They pay their rents on time. If they're a couple days late, there's a $40 late charge, no big deal. Things happen. I understand, but the way I am able to increase the value of the building so quickly is because rents were grossly below market. The building needed a lot of love. It needed a lot of energy and maintenance to get it to a particular class. I took a C-building to a B+ in a year. As that particular neighborhood happened to get better and better, in the next few years it might even be an A building in an A neighborhood. Then I've hit a home run. That's the reason why I really like the C buildings, C-'s or closer to D's, because you have such a large upside potential to get your money back quickly.

Invest Smart, Avoid The Appreciation Game

That is the name of the game. The name of the game is to get in, invest smart, invest for cash flow. Don't invest for appreciation. The market is always going up and down. You want to make sure your tenants are covering your mortgage, covering your expenses. The strategies that I have and have been using for years, they just work. The only reason I know they work is because they've worked for hundreds and hundreds well before me. It is not easy but it's very simple. You buy buildings based on the metrics. The metrics will let you know which direction to go, how and why and how fast. It's been incredible for me to see how this grows and how this can really change the way you sleep at night. When I know my buildings are taken care of, everything is secure, my tenants are happy, my family's happy, you just wake up in a different space.

I'm not sitting in this land of scarcity. I'm not sitting in this land of do I have enough? I am actively taking part in taking control over my financial future. I am actively trying to give back and to let kids know, young kids, 9, 10, 11, 12, kids know that there is a different way.

Nobody told me anything. They didn't teach me anything about this. I guarantee that as a 13, very ambitious little boy, if somebody would've said, "You could do A, B and C and this would maybe work," I would've definitely listened to them. I didn't have a lot of mentors when I was younger. I had a lot of coaches. I played lots of sports. My coaches taught me how to be a leader, how to be a captain, how to run the team.

That has helped me immensely in my business career, but I didn't have a financial mentor take me under their wing and say, "Listen Andy, you have a lot of potential and a lot of fire and a lot of drive. Let's maybe steer that towards this when you get a little bit older," anything. That's one of the reasons why I am so passionate about getting this message out there to help people and help other people's families. That is the reason why I love C and D buildings.

One More D Building Example

To circle back, I'll give you one more real-life scenario about a D building. This particular D building was a big, fat D-. It needed everything. It was almost falling down from termite damage. This particular building was a gigantic four-unit building. I mean, every single unit was a three-bedroom, two-bath. It was massive, massive, massive. Each one was almost 1,400 square feet, which basically means you have to rehab 4 small houses. Very expensive rehab and very stubborn tenants. These particular tenants had lived there for 20 years, I think one of them. I think the shortest one was 12 years. They weren't going anywhere. This was the kind of building that the particular seller couldn't deal with the tenants any longer. They weren't paying their bills. They weren't paying their mortgages. He was in a bad spot. I came in to help. We helped him out because he didn't want to deal with them anymore. We decided that it was worth the headache to take them on. We agreed to a price and we closed.

What Happens When Tenants Can't Transition Well

Once we became the new owners we knocked on the door, they slammed the door on our faces, "We're not paying you rent. We're not doing this." We had to slowly evict, over four months, all of the tenants. We successful did, as we always do. They didn't pay their rents. We followed the laws as the eviction process went on. We went to court and we won. Then the sheriff came, and we had to lock them out. They fought us all the way to the end. We even offered them money and we even offered to help them relocate and they refused. You have to really be a seasoned investor to take on this kind of project, but the upside to this D- property was we got it for a very, very good price. We were able to get it vacant within a time period that made sense for our investment schedule. We were able to invest hundreds of thousands of dollars in making these units beautiful.

This happened to be a D- property in an A neighborhood. We helped the neighborhood. We helped the neighbors. Believe me, the neighbors came out and clapped when these people finally left. These people were selling drugs out of this house. They weren't the kind of people that you want as your neighbors when you have kids playing in the front yard. We did the community a service, which made me feel great. For me, once we got this thing fully rehabbed, fully remodeled, and we marketed every single one of these units like it was its own house. It was a massive, massive property. There was a humongous courtyard in the middle that we made almost like a little park. We made a barbecue area for them. Each building had its own little fence, so it was like its own little house. We made these things gorgeous. When we marketed them, we marketed them to a very specific group that couldn't quite afford to live in the neighborhood because it was so expensive, but they wanted that neighborhood feel and have a large home. That's exactly what we did.

The Rewards of Adding Value

That particular property we will probably never sell. It's made so much money so fast that it's completely outperformed anything we could've ever, ever imagined. We were able to get our money back. We spent a ton of money in rehab. When we did do the refinance we got it back but it was just about a year and a half or so, so it took us a little bit longer to get our money back but; now we have this multimillion dollar piece of real estate that the cash that we put into the deal for the finance, for the rehab, for the materials, to pay for the property management company, to market it very heavily to the right, specific, perfect tenant, all the money we spent up front we recouped within 24 months, less than 24 months.

Lesson Learned

Now it's worth millions. Our price to get into the property was less than one million. Just to give you some context there, we have done really, really well. We did the community, again, a service. We made an eyesore of the neighborhood really nice. We took some of the drug activity out of the neighborhood. We cleaned up the area. As you get deeper and deeper into investing, I don't know, maybe it's just me but I really care about particular neighborhoods that I own properties in. I like to know that I'm being of service. That's a big reason why I'm writing this book. I enjoy being of service. I want to help people see what I didn't see. I want to help people know what I didn't know because it's possible. I promise you this, if you follow some simple steps and you are ridiculously and ruthlessly disciplined to your consistent efforts, your success will be amazing. Your success will be beyond your wildest dreams. You will be one of our success stories that we get to take a picture of you and put you on our wall and say, "They did it."

Chapter Eight:

THERE ARE TWO TYPES
OF MULTI-FAMILY REAL ESTATE INVESTING

Now that we've made the case for owning 100 Doors the question that is most frequently asked is "How do I get started?" There are many launching off points. You can start with a single-family home or if you have the capital you can jump with both feet in and buy a large 100-unit property. A journey of a thousand miles begin with the first step. Yet in the world of multi-unit investing banks see a significant difference in rental properties that are 1 – 4 units versus properties that are 5 units or more.

A Tale Of Two Different Rental Properties

As you get into the world of rental properties a line in the sand between 1-4 units is drawn rapidly. How banks perceive you, how property managers deal with you, and the ability to add value into the property to increase appreciation in the property all change. Why and investor would choose one over the author will depend on a number of factors. Let's delve deeper into the two types of rental properties showing some of the pros and cons.

Rental Properties 1-4 Units

When I began my journey on acquiring 100 Doors I started with a single-family home. The gentleman that introduced to Cleveland Ohio got me started on the single-family homes because it was simple to get started. It was little to no barriers to entry and it made too much sense, buy a house for $16,000 make $900/mo. in cash flow. This is how most people will get started on their 100 Doors journey.

It also just as easy to acquire a duplex, triplex, or a fourplex with just a little more effort and planning. There are multiple advantages to having more than one door on your property.

1 House Vs. 2-4 Units

Don't get me wrong if you can afford only a single-family home, start there by all means. Just keep in mind you want to graduate to multiple doors as quickly as possible. There are some distinct advantages and benefits.

Financing Is A Great Advantage

If you are going to through the hassle of financing a single-family home, you can simply apply the same loan application to get the biggest bang for your buck. a 2-4-unit investment property. The paperwork will be the same, but more importantly the FHA will help you acquire the property. The FHA and general lenders will treat 2-4 units as just like a single-family home when it comes to lending guidelines. The FHA may only require a 3-5% down payment and they will guarantee loans on a 4 unit up to $1.2 million dollars. Of course, there are special requirements to tap into that program, but it's worth every penny of it.

Economy of Scales

After acquiring all of my initial single-family homes I realized the nightmare scenario I had put myself in. Multiple tax bills, multiple insurance bills, multiple utility bills. Ridiculous.

When you have everything in one building, whether it's a 2,3 or 4-unit building, economy of scales kicks in quickly. You have one tax bill, you have one set of utility bills and any property repairs or expenses are a 2-way, three way, and/or four way split.

If someone moves out of a multi-unit, as opposed to a single-family home, you have another tenant or two or three covering the costs and still generating cash flow.

Liquidating Property

If you are planning to upgrade from single family home to a multi-unit it is very easy. You can find almost anyone to purchase a single-family home. Since this is the normal type of real estate transaction you have a great number people working on your behalf to make it happen. This is just not quite the case with multi-unit properties, no matter the size. The pool of buyers is much smaller for multi-units and can take longer than expected if you need a liquidation. This also works to your advantage when you are working to acquire mult-units, much less competition exists.

Rental Properties 5 Units and More

The magic of 5 units or more provides a level of control that can't be matched in the single-family investing world. You are able to increase cash flow, tap into depreciation, and master your expenses with precision.

Banks know and love this, so they really go out of their way to treat large multi-units with almost favored status. It's all by the numbers. Does the property cash flow? How much? and what potential value adds can you put into the deal? This is how commercial properties are treated across the board, just like a business, with heavy emphasis on what income does the property produce. This attitude also makes it easier to acquire or sell large multi-unit projects. It's a paint by the numbers scenario. If the price is right, if the rent rolls are transparent, and the property being purchased is classified properly (A, B, C, or D) then you can strategize very quickly on what you are willing to pay for the property and how you want to negotiate.

Economy of Scales

More units make it easier. It seems counter intuitive but as you increase the number of units you can put more systems in place. You can consolidate property management and you can increase your vendor relationships in unexpected ways. Electricians, maintenance crews, plumbers etc. all enjoy are large client and so your per unit expenses drop as you grow.

Lessons Learned

The 100 Doors concept doesn't discriminate against how you get involved in rental real estate. You have to get involved where your budget and comfort levels exists.

Chapter Nine:

THE 5 PILLARS
OF MULTI-UNIT INVESTING

"When I started my real estate career I jumped in with both feet. I hired mentors, took classes, went to live events, ect. I began working with investors right away and that is where I wanted to end up as fast as possible. Being an investor opens up a lot of opportunities for investing in businesses as well as Real Estate."

As I have progressed into a more buy and hold, income based strategy, rental income focus-I began to see what the full benefits are in being a true real estate investor, not just a real estate entrepreneur. Keep in mind nothing I mention here is meant to be construed as tax advice, consult with your account or attorney for that, as relayed to me, by people far smarter than I, are the five pillars of multi-unit investing: leverage, cash flow, equity build, appreciation (forced vs. demand), and Tax Benefits,

The First Pillar Of Multi-Unit Investing: Leverage

When I first learned about the concept of leverage I was getting my license to trade futures, options and forex. You would put down 3-5% on a futures contract, i.e. margin, and based on a second by second fluctuation you would gain or lose. Forex was even more significantly leveraged, 600 to 1.

So, I always had a frenetic vision of leverage, you never want to be exposed too long and at any moment fortune could turn against you and the leverage could be your worse enemy. In fact, during the mortgage during the mortgage collapse, it was the extended leverage that individuals took with the extended leverage that institutions took that lead to a financial crisis in the United States.

Leverage is defined as the "use of various financial instruments or borrowed capital to increase the potential return of an investment".

There is nothing sinister or even nefarious with the word leverage, too often times the word is made a synonym of "greed" and this is why it can sometimes backfire in practice.

Example Of Leverage

For an investment property, the bank will usually ask you to put down 25% of the purchase price. For easy math that's $20,000 on a $100,000 asset. The lender has provided most of the money and, yet you get to reap the rewards of owning the property. If the property appreciates by 5% in one year, $105,000, you would have a 20% return on your down payment, or basically your "Cash on Cash" return. If this increase happens every year, on your initial down payment, it could be a significant return.

Tapping into Leverage

Late night infomercials and online gurus have drummed it into our head that there are "no-money down" deals around every corner. Realistically they are few and far between, but owner's carrying notes back can be a significant help, the right borrower programs, such as the FHA, can help along with just having the down payment, alone or with partners or family. There is no need to overthink the situation. It's simply more important to find the deal, then work out the financing scenarios.

If you are purchasing the property as an investment, you may be in a position where your partners furnish some (or even all) of the money. Similarly, some sellers are willing to finance some of the purchase price of the property they wish to sell. Under such an arrangement, you can purchase a property with little money down and, in some cases, no money down at all.

The Second Pillar of Multi-Unit Investing: Cash Flow

When it comes to multi-unit investing it is optimal to think of monthly rents as bond payouts or dividends from blue chip stocks. If designed right, you will see monthly cash distributions that come back to you in the form of rent. By buying an asset that can be rented or leased out you are creating an income stream that affects your bottom line.

If you were to own a small 10-unit building, and each of the units generated $800 per month. Your gross would be $8,000 a month, minus 30% in expenses, you would have an additional $5,600 per month in net income or $67,200 dollars annually to service debt and or put in your pocket. If you set aside an average of 3% per month you would have a small reserve of $2,016.

This is the power of multi-unit investing. This is the power of owning 100 Doors.

Nothing Is Perfect

There are many things that will impact your cash flow amounts; vacancies, large unforeseen expenses that shoot past your reserves, carrying costs when you are improving or expanding on a piece of property. There are no magic bullets in investing, so you look for the largest number of benefits over negatives, and rental real estate has many.

The Third Pillar of Multi-Unit Investing: Equity Build

This is the most exciting component of multi-unit investing around. When you have "cash flow" and if you have used "leverage" to acquire that cash flow, every month your renters are paying down on your mortgage; principal and interest. So, your 30% in expenses do not all just evaporate, a portion of that is a forced savings back into your property, which in turn increases equity in the property, possibly setting you up for an opportunity to borrow against the equity, tax free.

The best property you can own is the property other people pay for on your behalf that you use other people's money to acquire.

The Fourth Pillar of Multi-Unit Investing: Appreciation (Demand versus Forced)

Appreciation is a pillar and is also the secret key to unlocking exceptional wealth from your multi-unit investing. Those that are solely familiar with appreciation that may happen with their home may think that true appreciation is an external activity. While they know they can remodel their property and have some gains, the largest gains come from an abundance of demand when only a few houses are available. In multi-unit real estate investing millions are made by "forcing" the appreciation.

Demand Appreciation

The old quote, "A rising tide lifts all ships", is an appropriate example of demand appreciation. When rental rates increase, and occupancy starts to go up in area overall, this phenomenon will positively impact your property as well. Your overall income increases, and the value of your location can move tremendously. As a rule of thumb though most demand appreciation occurs on the coasts while middle America tends to be more stable and income oriented. While there are bouts of demand driven activity in middle America, forced appreciation is both more reliable and more likely when you want to see an increase in property values.

Forced Appreciation

The great thing about forced appreciation is that you, the owner, of multi-unit properties are 100% in control of your value increases. Whenever you have more than 4 units on a property a whole set of economic assessments kicks in. Your property is evaluated by the income it produces not solely by it's cosmetics.

The easiest types of forced appreciation occur in one of three ways. First the owner can cut expenses and increase the take home income or second the owner can increase the rents to increase the overall income, or third an owner can do both. This typically happens when an owner buys right and is prepared to add value day one.

The rule of 10 applies when it comes to forced appreciation. For every value $1 increase in rent or decrease in expenses you increase the by $10. As you own a property and get better at operating it you will find various ways and opportunities to find the wasted dollars that will help you increase your properties value.

The Fifth Pillar Of Multi-Unit Investing: Tax Benefits

As you begin to sit down with your accountant or tax attorney you will find an innumerable number of tax advantages that I do not know or have a limited knowledge about. What I can say is that you will be pleasantly surprised at how accessible the tax code is to the real estate investor and what's available. I'm going to highlight just a few: depreciation, the 1031 exchange, and the ability to borrow out equity tax free.

The Power of Depreciation

As of this writing the IRS recognizes that an asset, like an apartment building, wears down. Based on this concept every year you get to take a 1/27.5 of its value off of your taxes. Now while this is just a paper loss, it can successfully offset your taxable income. To get more detailed information, look into downloading the IRS' booklet on Depreciation and Rental Property.

The Benefit of 1031 Exchange

Entire businesses and internet platforms have been built to help owners take advantage of the 1031 Exchange. For those that are familiar with doing it for your primary residence you may already be familiar with the power of this deferred exchange. What most don't know is that your multi-unit properties have the same 1031 exchange advantage. As long as you are not considered a fix and flip dealer, but a true real estate investor, holding property for 1 year or more, you will be able to use the 1031 exchange exemption on your taxes.

With a 1031 tax-free exchange you can:

Avoid capital gains tax

Avoid depreciation recapture tax`

Use 100% of the profits from the sale for next property

Never, Ever Sell Your Property

Don't ever sell any of your properties. The long-term benefits of tax avoidance, inter-generational wealth building, and asset building far outweigh the temporary need to fulfill a liquidity crunch. Savvy real estate investors simply borrow out the equity from the property, tax-free.

The benefits of this strategy are:

> NO tax paid on the cash from the refinance

> Future appreciation of rents and property value

> Tenants pay back the loan for you

> You ultimately hold on to a performing asset that could potentially do better.

This strategy only works when you maintain common sense. If you are incurring new debt on your property make sure that your cash flow still covers the expense, that you have a good low interest rate and long-time frame to repay it. This will mitigate any risk of overextending yourself.

Lesson Learned

These five pillars can each have a book on their own, nevertheless as a member of the 100 Doors Club you have an opportunity for true lifestyle planning. Planning that goes beyond just building a monthly income stream, planning that changes the way you perceive your whole life.

Chapter Ten:

UNDERSTANDING THE 10 YEAR REAL ESTATE CYCLE

In 1860 French economist and physician Clement Juglar identified the presence of economic cycles be between 8-11 years in length the study of economic or business cycles began around 1860. Since then there has been a consistent need to apply cycles to everything. I often wonder if this is a chicken and egg scenario. Did he really discover it or did his quantifying the phenomena force people to behave a certain way to create a self-fulfilling prophecy? Who knows for certain, but in the real estate world it is well known that a pattern of expansion and contraction is fairly consistent along a ten-year path.

The United States Is A Big Place

What is often little discussed or possibly even ignored is the fact that the United States is a huge place, comprised of 50 States and essentially 50 different economic cycles that ebb and flow at various times. North Dakota was once the hotbed of real estate activity.

The oil boom and increasing oil prices pushed North Dakota's property values up and rents into astronomical levels. Now that oil prices have declined, and the oil production has slowed down North Dakota is actually headed into a recession as of the writing of this book, with a $63 million shortfall in sales tax collection. This is telegraphing what to expect from the real estate tax collection and that environment overall in the long run. In fact, rents in many places have been cut in half and the reappraisal of these same properties is expected to not be too far behind.

On the flip side California has seen an explosive value increase in its property prices, bringing many areas close to their pre-mortgage backed security crisis price levels, pre-2008. While North Dakota is heading in to a downturn, California may be on the verge of one.

Everything Else In Between

As you take a peek through Zillow there are several states that simply have not yet recovered from the collapse of 2008 to 2010. Their property prices in many of their neighborhoods are approximately 50% of their 2008 levels, with only vague hints that they may go up in price in some distant future. Cleveland, Ohio is one such city. As you look at what the estimated value of the house should be and what it is selling for there is a significant discrepancy in many instances. You find this issue particularly in the duplex, triplex, and fourplex areas-small commercial.

Foreclosures, Auctions, & Neighborhood Comparables

What you see is not what you get in this instance. While you may see a cash flowing duplex that should be selling for two to three times the asking offer, they are not because these small commercial properties are suffering from being appraised like their single-family home counterparts. This means that every foreclosure or property that goes to auction is dragging down the price of the properties we like to typically take down. It helps when you are a cash buyer, it helps when you want to build a big real estate portfolio fast. Unfortunately, this also diminishes your access to capital from the banks because they may still be seeing the property as earlier in the 10-year real estate all the while rents are increasing, and the local economy is developing.

Calculating the True Value of a Rental Property

Whether you use Cap Rate (Net Annual Income/ Purchase price), Cash On Cash Return (Net Annual Income/Total Money Invested), Gross Rent Multiplier (Sales Price/Annual Gross Rents), or a simple House Value (Multiplier X Annual Gross Rents) to arrive at the true value of an income producing asset, the banks won't accept those numbers as adding value to small commercials appraisal.

In fact, the bank is more concerned about the properties curb appeal and how it stacks up against local single-family homes, with little regard to the rental income being brought in. This is an unfortunate scenario in Cleveland, Ohio that is happening as of this writing. Appraisers and banks are being hyper conservative in how they appraise income properties, for purchase as well refinancing. While not perfect, this is a far cry from my early experiences of "no" banks' lending in Cleveland at all. So, this is a sign that Cleveland, Ohio is just starting their new 10-year cycle, coming off of the lows of the end of their last 10-year cycle.

Nothing New Under The Sun

Every real estate cycle has had different reasons why they have exploded. In 1983 to 1988 tax incentives along with excess capital allowed for the housing market to boom. From 1993 to 1998 the digital economy took off. We saw the real estate cycle of 2003 to 2008 take off because of easy access to capital, mortgage backed securities, and a booming stock market. This cycle of 2013 to 2018 is heavily dependent on healthcare, authenticity and internet/technology. Various areas around the country are poised to take advantage of these trends and many more. Keeping your eyes peeled for real estate opportunities in these sectors; along with data centers, public infrastructure, alternative energy, vertical and micro farming, will give you the chance to join the beginning of the 10-year cycle almost anywhere.

Real Estate Cycles Are A Continuous Rolling Loop

When you look at any real estate cycle chart there is an ebb and flow of boom and bust activity. One recession period rolls into the beginning of a boom period, which moves up along a good trajectory, until it tops out and begins it's rapid descent once again. Knowing how each phase of the real estate cycles is key to understanding how best to approach the market. By being nimble and focused there are opportunities at any phase.

The First Phase: Recovery

While we can start at any point on the rolling real estate cycle, we will begin the most basic, the recovery period after a boom and bust period. During this time rentals are sluggish or are priced low. Overall the rental rate is flat, not much activity is going on and it seems as if the market is still in a recession. This is the most difficult phase of the cycle to identify because the spirit of the most recent bust looms heavy on the market. This also the time to be strategic in your approach. For the strong hearted there are several ways to get on the board during this period. You can find inexpensive real estate to either buy and hold or do light rehab to make rent ready. You can hunt out ongoing rented properties and look for "value add" scenarios to force appreciate the property. This is where the money is made in real estate, buying right.

The Second Phase: Expansion

This part of the cycle is easy to spot. There is a vibe in the air. More access to capital begins to exist, rents are increasing, more applications per vacancy shows up. Prices are going up, but are reasonably priced to property value. We also are seeing one or more industries increasing their hiring. This is the time to look for D properties in a C area, C properties in a B area, B properties in an A area. This will be the most bang for your buck and set you up for the third and fourth phases.

The Third Phase: Hyper Supply

This is the time ill prepared landlords sell their properties and put pressure on the market actually helping push the market into the Fourth Phase: Recession. Better prepared landlords hunker down and come up with strategies to make their current tenants happy to retain them longer or put newer tenants into long term leases. Whatever the case this is the moment in which supply exceeds demand. A change in economy, too much new construction or too many successful value add rehabs have gone up and a pressure on rent prices begins.

The Fourth Phase: Recession

This is when the 1-month free rent specials come out in droves. Supply officially out paces demand. Property vacancies increase significantly and an overall halt to new construction, property improvements, and property acquisitions. The time to start bargain shopping has begun again.

Lesson Learned

Each one of these phases can last in differing amounts along the ten-year cycle. Some can last for years, while other phases come and go, transitioning rapidly to the next phase. By being aware of the 10-year cycle and the four phases that exist within it, you will begin to pay closer attention to the real estate market and come up with strategies that are appropriate to you and the area you may be investing in.

Chapter Eleven:

NOT IN YOUR
OWN BACKYARD

Over the past 3 ½ years I have met investors that are investing in Tennessee, Florida, Georgia, and Texas all in a big way. Whether they are buying and flipping multiple homes or building huge syndicates to buy large apartment complexes each of these investors also found something about their areas that resonated with them.

Once a month we have a 100 Doors Facebook Live meeting and I give examples and situations for viewers to learn. I have taken some of the same information from those meetings and give it to you here because I wanted to use this chapter to show you how you can find various other areas to invest in if you want to simply "paint by the numbers" with your real estate investing.

If you wish to attend one of our events just sign up for Andy Dane Carter's, "Live 4 Free", private Facebook group at andydancecarter.com

Classic Indicators To Use To Determine Where To Buy Real Estate

There are multiple resources available to investors online to give them a clear picture of what is happening around the country. RealtyTrac has a lot of data, the US Census Bureau, and CoreLogic to name a few.

What you want to be able to analyze are the following data points:

• Population Growth

• Primarily from Net Migration

• States With Large and Growing Populations

• Workforce

• Income Growth

• Educated Workforce

• GDP/GSP

• Diversified Economic Base

• Good Debt Rating

• RE Cycle Phase

• Real Estate Prices Not Volatile

I won't go over "ALL" of the data points above, but we will take a couple quick statistical snapshots to see how people use the numbers to make their decisions. Here is a map of last year's census on fastest growing states. The west coast sees a staggering population change in fact making Utah the fastest growing state in the nation. There is also a heavy population increase in the south east with Florida leading the pack. Unfortunately, those same areas are also going through a boom cycle in the real estate market. They are heading into the end of their 10-year cycle, with many people anticipating some type of collapse in southern California.

Following Utah, Nevada (2.0 percent), Idaho (1.8 percent), Florida (1.8 percent) and Washington (1.8 percent) saw the largest percentage increases in population.

North Dakota, which had been the fastest-growing state for the previous four years, mostly from people moving into the state, fell out of the top ten in growth due to a net outflow of migrants to other parts of the country. Its growth slowed from 2.3 percent in the previous year to 0.1 percent.

Nationally, the U.S. population grew by 0.7 percent to 323.1 million. Furthermore, the population of voting-age residents, adults age 18 and over, grew to 249.5 million, making up 77.2 percent of the population in 2016, an increase of 0.9 percent from 2015 (247.3 million).

Eight states lost population between July 1, 2015, and July 1, 2016, including Pennsylvania, New York and Wyoming, all three of which had grown the previous year. Illinois lost more people than any other state (-37,508).

Checking Out Population Growth

It's interesting to see Ohio in the top 10 Most Populous States.

Top 10 Most Populous States: 2016				
Rank	Name	2010	2015	2016
1	California	37,254,522	38,993,940	39,250,017
2	Texas	25,146,100	27,429,639	27,862,596
3	Florida	18,804,592	20,244,914	20,612,439
4|	New York	19,378,110	19,747,183	19,745,289
5	Illinois	12,831,574	12,839,047	12,801,539
6	Pennsylvania	12,702,857	12,791,904	12,784,227
7	Ohio	11,536,727	11,605,090	11,614,373
8	Georgia	9,688,680	10,199,398	10,310,371
9	North Carolina	9,535,688	10,035,186	10,146,788
10	Michigan	9,884,129	9,917,715	9,928,300

		Top 10 States in Numeric Growth: 2015 to 2016			
Rank	Name	2010	2015	2016	Numeric change
1	Texas	25,146,100	27,429,639	27,862,596	432,957
2	Florida	18,804,592	20,244,914	20,612,439	367,525
3	California	37,254,522	38,993,940	39,250,017	256,077
4	Washington	6,724,545	7,160,290	7,288,000	127,710
5	Arizona	6,392,301	6,817,565	6,931,071	113,506
6	North Carolina	9,535,688	10,035,186	10,146,788	111,602
7	Georgia	9,688,680	10,199,398	10,310,371	110,973
8	Colorado	5,029,324	5,448,819	5,540,545	91,726
9	Oregon	3,831,072	4,024,634	4,093,465	68,831
10	South Carolina	4,625,410	4,894,834	4,961,119	66,285

		Top 10 States in Numeric Growth: 2015 to 2016			
Rank	Name	2010	2015	2016	Percent change
1	Utah	2,763,888	2,990,632	3,051,217	2.03
2	Nevada	2,700,691	2,883,758	2,940,058	1.95
3	Idaho	1,567,650	1,652,828	1,683,140	1.83
4	Florida	18,804,592	20,244,914	20,612,439	1.82
5	Washington	6,724,545	7,160,290	7,288,000	1.78
6	Oregon	3,831,072	4,024,634	4,093,465	1.71
7	Colorado	5,029,324	5,448,819	5,540,545	1.68
8	Arizona	6,392,301	6,817,565	6,931,071	1.66
9	District of Columbia	601,766	670,377	681,170	1.61
10	Texas	25,146,100	27,429,639	27,862,596	1.58

During 2017, the Census Bureau will release estimates of the 2016 population of counties, cities and towns, and metropolitan and micropolitan statistical areas as well as national, state and county population estimates by age, sex, race and Hispanic origin. Population estimates for Puerto Rico and its municipios by age and sex will be released as well.

What Makes Cleveland Ohio So Unique to Invest

If it made sense to buy multi-unit properties here in Southern California I would have. Here is an example I pulled right off of LoopNet. A 3.79% cap rate on $2.6 million dollars. There are only 11 units so any of the value add activities we would attempt; increase rents or decrease expenses. There is just not enough wiggle room with number of units here. Add to the fact that $2.6milliion dollars would put you in the hundred unit + range in the Midwest with a lot of value add opportunity.

11 unit Apt Bldg

• Active

$2,595,000

11,380 SF

11

3.79%

Multifamily
Garden/Low-Rise

Attending Our Field Trips With Us

As of this writing I have taken one set of investors on a property buying trip to Cleveland Ohio.

The goal is to make these trips five times a year. By putting their boots on the ground, they can see the property development, and our team of partners that we work with.

Map Of Rental Yields Across The Country

Ohio is right in the highest area of the country

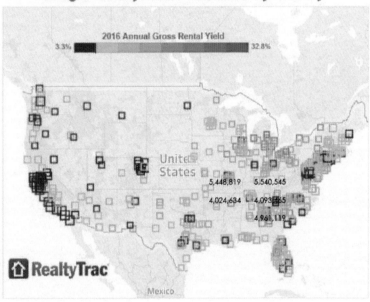

Map Of Cleveland Ohio

Quick Ohio Facts

Ohio is the 34th largest by area, the 7th most populous, and the 10th most densely populated of the 50 United States. The state's capital and largest city is Columbus. The state takes its name from the Ohio River.

- 95% housing occupancy rate in downtown Cleveland (Downtown Cleveland Alliance, 2104) Cleveland is among the Top 10 job markets for new college graduates – (CNN)

- Northeast Ohio is one of the hottest entrepreneur regions in the nation – (Entrepreneur)

- Cleveland serves as headquarters to 11 companies on the Fortune 500 list, both industrial and non-industrial, including National City Corp., Eaton Corp., Parker Hannifin Corp.,

Sherwin-Williams Co., KeyCorp, Nacco Industries, American Greetings Corp., Ferro Corp., Medical Mutual of Ohio, Applied Industries Technologies, and Lincoln Electric Holdings (City- Data.com)

- Home to 27 area colleges and universities
- Regional Banking Hub: home to one of 12 Federal Reserve Banks
- Home to four professional sports teams
- Home of the Rock-n-Roll Hall of Fame with 7+ million visitors
- University Hospitals named one of nation's best hospitals – (U.S. News & World Report)
- Home of the nation's first Medical Mart
- Cleveland is a Health Care Hub with over 60 Hospitals and a big Biomedical Industry
- The Biomedical industry is a large exporter of goods adding further financial gain to the community.
- Cleveland is now home to over 600 biomedical facilities with more being added each year.
- Northeast Ohio economy has consistently grown and outpaced the national average for job growth.
- They have assembled a team to Chambers of Commerce and affiliates to help obtain this growth, a team known as Team NEO

- Ohio Tax reform has attracted businesses and produced a low cost of living environment.

- Since 2007, the organization has attracted more than 20 new companies, 2,200 new jobs and more than $70M in annual payroll

- Corporate friendly tax structure

- Low cost of living

- Northeast Ohio is home to 300 foreign-owned businesses,

- The region is a hub for food processing, where major brands such as Smucker's, Nestlé, and Pierre Foods

- 5 interstate highways

- 6 deep water ports, 3 class 1 railroads, 2 international airports create low cost logistics

- 29 colleges and universities

- 2 million talented workers create a smart productive multi-cultural workforce.

- Cleveland low acquisition costs are able to provide returns as high as 15 and 20% cap rates. Cleveland is a great investment location for those seeking strong cash flow.

BONUS CHAPTER

100 DOORS FOR VETERANS

A LITTLE

GUIDANCE FOR U.S. VETERANS

When I sat down to write this book a good friend of mine, a former Navy medic, fell on hard times and I volunteered to help him navigate his way through the system just, so he could get his benefits and find out how he could get assistance just to find a place to live. It was heartbreaking and frustrating. Someone who did their service to their country was honorably discharged, but couldn't receive the most basic resources to live, without jumping through hoops.

I had this section of the book created by a researcher. As I learn more on how to help veterans and their families achieve financial independence this section will grow and hopefully become it's own book. I hope some of this information helps.

1.0 Financial Guidance, Protections, & Assistance

1.1 Pension benefits for veterans:

Veterans with low incomes who are permanently and totally disabled, or are age 65 and older, may be eligible for monetary support if they have 90 days or more of active military service, at least one day of which was during a period of war. If the active duty occurred after September 7, 1980, you must have served at least 24 months or the full period that you were called up (with some exceptions). The Veteran's discharge must have been under conditions other than dishonorable and the disability must be for reasons other than the Veteran's own willful misconduct.

Pension benefit payments are made to bring the Veteran's total income, including other retirement or Social Security income, to a level set by Congress.

1.2 Aid and Attendance Pension Benefits

If you qualify for a VA pension and you have a disability that meets certain criteria, you may also be eligible to receive an Aid and Attendance (A&A) or Housebound benefit. For more information on applying for A&A or Housebound benefits contact your local VA Regional Office.

1.3 Bonuses

Veterans who were living in Massachusetts immediately prior to entering the armed forces may be eligible for a one-time, tax-free, bonus from the Commonwealth. If the Veteran is deceased, his or her family may be eligible for this bonus. Veterans who are unable to complete the required period of service because of injury or illness caused or aggravated during their service are generally still eligible.

2.0 Housing Resources

2.1 State-aided Public Housing

- ✓ Veterans (see Definitions section) applying for state-aided public housing through a local housing authority, who are to be displaced by any low-rent housing project or by a public slum clearance or urban renewal project or who were displaced within three years prior to applying for low-rent housing, when equally in need and eligible for occupancy as other applicants, shall be given preference in tenant selection in the following order:
- ✓ Families of disabled Veterans whose disability has been determined by the U.S. Department of Veterans Affairs to be service-connected.

- ✓ Families of deceased Veterans whose death has been determined by the U.S. Department of Veterans Affairs to be service-connected.

- ✓ Families of all other Veterans.

- ✓ The word "Veteran" shall also include the spouse, surviving spouse, dependent parent or child of a Veteran, and the guardian of a child of a Veteran. In communities where, low-income family housing does not exist, preference in admission shall be given to Veterans for all scattered site housing units acquired by a local housing authority. In determining the net income for the purpose of computing the rent of a totally unemployable disabled Veteran, a housing authority shall exclude amounts of disability compensation paid by the United States government for disability occurring in connection with military service in excess of $1800.

2.2 Foreclosures

Where the SCRA is applicable, mortgage lenders may not foreclose upon, or seize property for a failure to pay a mortgage debt while a Service member is on active duty or within 90 days after the period of military service unless they have the approval of a court. To obtain permission from the court to foreclose, the lender would have to show that the Service member's ability to repay the debt was not affected by his or her military service.

To learn more about the Justice Department's enforcement of laws protecting Servicemembers, visit www.Servicemembers.gov. If you believe your rights under the SCRA have been violated, contact your nearest Armed Forces Legal Assistance Office http:// legalassistance.law.af.mil/content/locator.php.

2.3 Termination of Residential, Business and Other Leases

A Servicemember who signed a lease for residential, professional, business, agricultural, or similar purposes is entitled to terminate that lease if he or she enters active military service after signing the lease. A Servicemember who signed a lease after entering active military service can terminate that lease if he or she receives orders for a permanent change of station or to deploy with a military unit for at least 90 days. To terminate a lease, the Servicemember must provide the landlord or other lessor with at least 30 days' written notice of the termination and a copy of the Service member's military orders.

2.4 Homelessness

The Massachusetts Department of Veterans' Services contracts with several nonprofit organizations in order to provide housing for eligible homeless Veterans. Housing services include Emergency Homeless Shelters, group residences, and Single Room Occupancy (SRO) quarters. Housing services are provided for male and female Veterans. All residences maintain a sober, drug-free environment. For more information, visit the Services and List of Providers pages of the Department of Veterans' Services website, www.mass.gov/Veterans. A list of Massachusetts homeless shelters for Veterans is provided in Appendix C.

The VA maintains a 24/7 national call center and online chat service for Veterans and their families who are homeless or at-risk of becoming homeless. To learn more about VA homeless programs and mental health services in your area, call or chat online with a trained VA counselor: 1-877-4AID-VET (1-877-424-3838) or http://www. va.gov/HOMELESS/index.asp.

2.5 Soldiers' Homes

Massachusetts Soldiers' Homes provide a variety of services to Veterans such as acute hospital care, domiciliary care, long-term care, physical and occupational therapy, laboratory and radiology services, an outpatient department, and a social services department. There are two state Soldiers' Homes, one in Chelsea, the other in Holyoke. For information on eligibility and admission, contact:

Chelsea Soldiers' Home
91 Crest Avenue
Chelsea, MA 02150
617-884-5660

2.6 VA Home Loan Guaranty

The U.S. Department of Veterans Affairs (VA) home loan program provides a guaranty of payment to servicers issuing home mortgage loans to Veterans. For VA housing loan purposes, the term "Veteran" includes certain members of the Selected Reserve, active duty service personnel and certain categories of spouses. To find out if you are eligible visit the "Home Loan Guaranty Services" section of the VA website at: http://benefits.va.gov/homeloans/. If a lender cannot verify a Veteran's eligibility electronically, the Veteran can apply for a Certificate of Eligibility by submitting a completed VA Form 26-1880, Request Certificate of Eligibility, with proof of military service, to:

Atlanta Regional Loan Center
Attn: COE (262)
P. O. Box 100034
Decatur, GA 30031

3.0 Medical Care & Death

3.1 SCRA & Health Insurance

Under the Servicemembers Civil Relief Act (SCRA), Servicemembers whose health insurance lapses or is terminated during their military service are entitled to reinstatement of that insurance upon leaving the military. The Servicemember may not be subjected to a waiting period, coverage limitations because of the lapse in coverage. These protections also apply to dependents such as children or spouses, covered under the Servicemember's policy.

The SCRA also does not cover health insurance provided by a Servicemember's employer. Employer-provided insurance is covered under the Uniformed Services Employment and Reemployment Rights Act (USERRA).

3.2 Veterans Affairs Health Care

Many Veterans are eligible to receive health care from the U.S. Department of Veterans Affairs. Eligibility for most VA benefits is based upon discharge from active military service under other than dishonorable conditions, and service-connected disability rating, status as a recent combat Veteran, receipt of certain medals (e.g. Purple Heart), or income.

"Active military service" means full-time service, other than active duty for training, as a member of the Army, Navy, Air Force, Marine Corps, Coast Guard, or as a commissioned officer of the Public Health Service, Environmental Science Services Administration or National Oceanic and Atmospheric Administration. Reservists and National Guard members who were called to active duty by the federal government are generally also eligible for VA health care if they meet the other requirements. Dishonorable and bad conduct discharges may make a Veteran ineligible. Some family members of Veterans are eligible for VA benefits as well.

3.3 Medicare

Medicare is a health insurance program for people age 65 or older, some disabled people under age 65, and people of all ages with

end-stage renal disease (permanent kidney failure treated with dialysis or a transplant). Medicare has three parts. Medicare Part A is hospitalization insurance which may cover critical care such as inpatient hospital stays. Medicare Part B is medical insurance which may pay for more routine medical care such as doctor's visits and lab tests. Medicare Part D covers some prescription drugs. If you are over 65 years old there may be no cost for Medicare Part A if you have paid Medicare taxes on your income throughout your life.

3.4 TRICARE for Life

TRICARE for Life is a benefit available to retired U.S. Military and their families. It encompasses the processing of all TRICARE claims for services rendered to individuals who have dual eligibility under both TRICARE and Medicare. The Defense Enrollment

Eligibility Reporting System (DEERS) is a military database that lists everyone who is eligible for TRICARE benefits. Make sure your DEERS record is up-to-date. This will help us process your claims quickly and accurately. If you are not sure if you are eligible, please contact DEERS at 1-800-538-9552 for more information about your eligibility on their system. If you have both A&B, you are eligible for Tricare for Life. If you only have Part A, your sponsor must be active duty. If you only have part B, you must be 65 or older and not be entitled to premium-free Medicare part A. For coverage and payment information please visit the TRICARE for Life website at www. tricare4u.com.

4.0 Life Insurance

Under the SCRA, certain life insurance policies are entitled to special protection. To obtain this protection the insured Servicemember, or his or her representative, must submit an application to the insurance company for protection under the SCRA. The insurance company will then submit a request to the Secretary of Veterans Affairs for approval. Approved policies are guaranteed by the United States and cannot lapse or be terminated for failure to pay premiums or interest after the date when the Secretary receives the application. The protection provided by the SCRA is limited to a maximum policy amount, and applies during the insured's period of military service and for two years thereafter. In order to qualify, the policy must:

1. Be whole life, endowment, universal life, or term insurance

2. Not decrease the amount of coverage or require the payment of an additional amount as premiums if the insured engages in military service (except increases in premiums in individual term insurance based upon age); or

3. Not limit or restrict coverage for any activity required by military service; and///

4. Be in force for at least 180 days before the date of the insured's entry into military service and at the time of application.

To find out if you have a policy that is entitled to this protection, contact your life insurance company and ask them to assist you with the application process.

5.0 Survivors Pension

The Survivors Pension benefit, which may also be referred to as Death Pension, is a tax free monetary benefit payable to a low-income, un-remarried surviving spouse and / or unmarried children of a deceased Veteran with wartime service.

5.1 Eligibility

The deceased Veteran must have met the following service requirements:

- For service on or before September 7, 1980, the Veteran must have served at least 90 days of active military service, with at least one day during a war time period.

- If he or she entered active duty after September 7, 1980, generally he or she must have served at least 24 months or the full period for which called or ordered to active duty with at least one day during a war time period.

- Was discharged from service under other than dishonorable conditions. While an un-remarried spouse is eligible at any age, a child of a deceased wartime Veteran must be:

- Under 18, OR

- Under age 23 if attending a VA-approved school, OR

- Permanently incapable of self-support due to a disability before age 18

Your yearly family income must be less than the amount set by Congress to qualify for the Survivors Pension benefit. Learn more about income and net worth limitation, and see an example of how VA calculates the Survivors Pension benefit.